Composting When It Counts

Homestead-Scale Composting You Can Depend On

Noah Sanders

"So he said to the man who took care of the vineyard, 'For three years now I've been coming to look for fruit on this fig tree and haven't found any. Cut it down! Why should it use up the soil?' 'Sir,' the man replied, 'leave it alone for one more year, and I'll dig around it and fertilize it. If it bears fruit next year, fine! If not, then cut it down.'" (Luke 13:7–9, NIV 1984)

And my God will meet all your needs according to his glorious riches in Christ Jesus. (Philippians 4:19, NIV 1984)

Composting When it Counts by Noah Sanders
© 2024 by Noah Sanders
All Rights Reserved

Published by Rora Valley Publishing
www.roravalleypublishing.com

ISBN: 978-0-9851315-6-2

Contains material from The Well-Watered Garden Handbook, Second Edition, copyright 2023, by Noah Sanders

Acknowledgments go to Darryl Edwards, Hazel Edwards, and Foundations for Farming International.

TABLE OF CONTENTS

INTRODUCTION

Do you have more than enough compost for your homestead? As we look at our fragile food system in America, many of us are relying on our gardens for a resilient source of food for our family. But for that to be a long-term solution we must produce our own soil fertility.

Most homesteaders know that compost is the secret to growing our own fruits and vegetables without dependency on chemical fertilizers. But the average backyard compost system doesn't produce enough volume of compost consistently to rely on it for your family's food production. In this booklet you will be given a simple, powerful, and proven composting technique that will enable you to create living soil and produce abundant crops.

With only a few simple supplies and materials you can find on your own homestead, you can master the art of homestead-scale compost production to ensure your homestead feeds you and your family no matter what comes in the future.

OVERVIEW OF THE METHOD IN THIS BOOKLET

What is this booklet about?

This booklet has been compiled to give a simple method of thermal composting for serious gardeners and homesteaders. Most backyard compost systems are insufficient to produce enough compost to sustain a serious garden. The method taught in this booklet enables large quantities of living compost to be produced on a homestead using locally available materials. This can reliably produce yields in a family's garden season after season without any purchased inputs.

What is thermal compost?

Compost is decomposed organic matter teeming with beneficial microorganisms that acts as a fertilizer factory to feed plants. Thermal compost is made by providing ideal conditions for aerobic decomposition with a minimum four feet size pile, good moisture management, and timely turning. This results in high temperatures for neutralizing pathogens and weed seeds and a consistent, high-quality compost ready for use in 8 weeks.

Where did this compost system come from?

This method is based on the techniques taught by Dr. Elaine Ingham, recognized as one of the world's foremost soil biologists. It was adapted by Darryl and Hazel Edwards of Foundations for Farming in Zimbabwe Africa into a simple method that can be easily taught to the poorest farmer. The author of this booklet was trained in Zimbabwe.

What is required for making thermal compost?

All that is required to make thermal compost is waste organic matter like leaves and grass, a nitrogen source like manure or legumes, six stakes for corner posts, 2 barrels or water troughs for holding water, a stiff wire for monitoring temperature, a wheelbarrow, and a hoe, shovel, or garden fork for turning the pile. You will also need an area for stockpiling materials and a site for building your pile.

How do you make it?

In brief, take your materials, dunk them in water in the barrel, and place inside four posts spaced 4 ft apart. Mix any manure with water in a wheelbarrow before adding. Add layers of material in the appropriate ratios until the pile is 4 ft tall. Monitor the temperature and turn at least once a week for 8 weeks. The compost is now ready to use.

Who is this appropriate for?

Thermal compost is a good option for replacing chemical fertilizers for the serious backyard gardener, community garden, or homestead. One 4x4x4 ft pile will be enough for a ¼ acre of corn or a medium size vegetable garden. Due to the material and space needed thermal compost is not always possible for small backyard gardeners.

What examples of success are there?

This method is being used all over Africa through the trainings of Foundations for Farming. In combination with Conservation Agriculture techniques and the Pfumvudza model, small scale farmers are achieving food security without needing purchased inputs. Through Redeeming the Dirt Noah Sanders has been promoting and teaching this same method with great results to many gardeners and homesteaders.

Compost Links:

Video of Compost Making:	Article on Pfumvudza:

UNDERSTANDING HOW COMPOST WORKS

How Does Compost Work?

To fully appreciate and master the art of compost making we need to understand how the soil naturally feeds plants in natural creation. Let's take a look at some of the major components of healthy soil and how they work together.

The components of healthy soil

There are three major unique components of healthy soil that you may have observed.

1. <u>Minerals:</u> Dead things that were never alive
2. <u>Organic Matter:</u> Dead things that were once alive
3. <u>Micro-organisms</u>: Living things that are still alive

<u>Minerals: Dead things that were never alive</u>

Minerals are the base component of the soil that varies depending on your region. You don't really get to pick your minerals. But they each have different characteristics and their own pros and cons. Most soils contain a blend of these minerals with one being the predominant component.

- **Sand:** Sand is comprised of relatively large particles of minerals. For comparison think of a sand particle as a large book like a dictionary. Sand is easy to work and drains well, but it also dries out quickly and leaches nutrients.
- **Silt:** Silt is made up of small particles of minerals. For comparison think of them as a small booklet like this manual. Silt is easy to work and holds water and nutrients better than sand, but it can still compact or wash away because of the light particles.

- **Clay:** Clay is made up of VERY small particles of minerals. For comparison think of them as a single page in a book. Clay holds water and nutrients very well, but it can have trouble with compacting, not draining water, and erosion.

Organic Matter: Dead things that were once alive.

Organic matter is composed of the dead material from leaves, sticks, grasses, roots, digested plants (manure), and dead bugs and microbes. This material provides food for soil microbes, and they decompose it into what is known as humus and humic acid, both of which help to balance out the negative attributes of soil minerals. For example, humus helps sand to hold water and nutrients better while also helping clay to drain and not compact.

Micro-organisms: Living things that are still alive

Healthy soil is full of life. There are more microbes in a teaspoon of healthy soil than there are people on the planet! Two of the major categories of micro-organisms that are helpful to know about are bacteria and fungi.

- *Bacteria* are small, single celled organisms that can rapidly multiply and feed on minerals and organic matter, making nutrients available to plants. They love to feed on **sugars** present in the soil around the roots of plants and in fresh decomposing plant material. They also need **nitrogen** in order to reproduce and grow.

- *Fungi* are organisms that grow and create networks of fungal strands throughout the soil. They feed on minerals and especially love **brown, woody** organic matter like fallen logs and fall leaves. They can transport nutrients through their fungal networks and trade it with different plants. One fungal organism in Oregon covers 2,384 acres[1].

The Structure of Healthy Soil

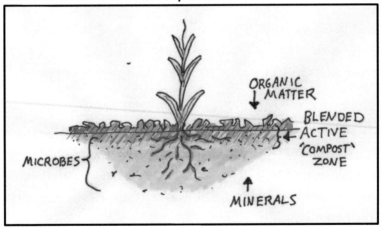

If you wanted to build a house and only gave the builders a list of the materials, you might not get a house that functions the way you want it to. A house is defined not only by its components, but by its *structure*. The same is true of the soil. Healthy soil is

---

[1]   https://www.scientificamerican.com/article/strange-but-true-largest-organism-is-fungus/

held together by humic acid and is full of channels left by micro-organisms and roots that have rotted. It is like a sponge and holds water through capillary action without being saturated. Healthy soil can be up to 70% air by volume! This water and air are necessary for sustaining the life in the soil. The soil is also comprised of layers, or strata, and is not a homogeneous potting mixture. The upper layers are primarily organic matter and the lower you go the more they are composed of minerals. Different microbes like to live in different layers. Bacteria that like oxygen live near the surface and bacteria that don't like sunlight or need oxygen live in lower layers.

How Does Healthy Soil Work?

When we harvest crops from our garden, we are taking nutrients away that we need to replace. Some of the major nutrients that our plants need are:

- Nitrogen: Helps leaf growth.
- Phosphorus: Helps root growth.
- Potassium: Helps with plant health.
- Micronutrients: Works with other nutrients.

Conventional agriculture supplies these nutrients through salt-based chemical fertilizers that are available directly to the plants. But there are also other factors that affect the ability for these nutrients to be available to the plant. You can have fertilizer in the ground but that doesn't mean the plants can always use it.

Factors affecting Nutrient Uptake:

- Soil PH
- Soil Compaction
- Soil moisture
- Soil temp
- Soil organic matter

So how do we remedy these?

- Plowing, burning, and chemicals **negatively** affect factors.
- Minimal tillage, mulch, and compost **benefit** these factors.

Nature doesn't get yearly applications of chemical fertilizer, so how does it get fed?

A Natural Fertilizer Factory

In nature the soil is an amazing 'fertilizer factory' composed of an incredible community of plants, bugs, bacteria, fungi, and other micro-organisms all working together.

Plants feed themselves using sunlight to make sugar through the miraculous process known as 'photosynthesis'. They use this sugar as a building block to build the plant. 40% of the sugars they use to build the part of the plant you see and 30% goes to the roots. Where does the other 30% go? The plant puts it into the soil around the roots to attract the microbes and bacteria that like to feed on sugar. The benefit to the plant is that the bacteria are also feeding on decaying plant material and minerals that contain nutrients the plant can't access directly. But as the bacteria feeds some of the nutrients pass through their bodies as waste or is released from their bodies when they die and are eaten by something else. This creates a gradual release of valuable nutrients that is in a form the plants can utilize. This is similar to the way that cows eat grass (which we can't eat) and turn the nutrients into a form that we can eat (like milk or steak).

There are many other facets to this amazing fertilizer factory in the soil and it is said that we know more about outer space than we do about the soil. But the beauty is that we don't have to understand how it all works to benefit from it. All we have to do is create the right

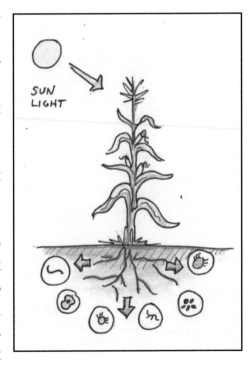

conditions and it will establish itself.

One of the reasons plowing and tilling is so detrimental is because they disrupt this living community in the soil and create the need for chemical fertilizers. Chemical fertilizers disrupt this system as well since they reduce the need for the plant to partner with the microbes and their salt-base is detrimental to the microbes. This results in the soil developing a dependency on chemical fertilizer over time and needing more and more to get the same result.

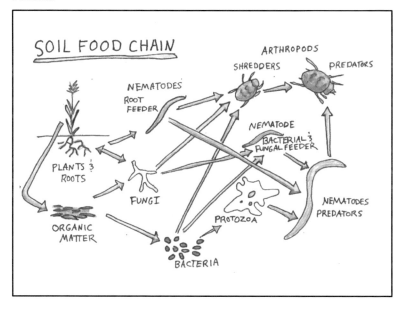

If we just minimize soil disturbance and put a nice blanket of organic matter (mulch) on the top it creates the ideal conditions for the soil to re-establish its natural fertilizer factory. But how do we help speed up the healing process and give generously to the soil when we are harvesting from it? There are two main tools we can use.

1. Compost brings organic matter and microbes back into the soil to re-establish or boost the natural fertilizer factory of microbes that feed the plant.
2. Natural fertilizers are liquid solutions rich in natural nutrients that we can use to feed the plants directly when they need a boost without the negative effects of chemical fertilizers.

A Foundation of Compost

As I mentioned earlier, the solid ingredients of healthy soil (other than water and air) include three major categories:

- **Local minerals** (clay, sand, silt. i.e. dead material that was never alive)
- **Organic matter** (rotted leaves, plants, bugs i.e. dead material that was once alive)
- **Microorganisms** (bacteria and fungi, i.e. living things that are still alive!)

Most poor soils contain minerals but lack both organic matter and a healthy population of microorganisms. *Good compost is a combination of these two lacking ingredients.* It is decayed organic matter teeming with microorganisms. It is not fertilizer. It is nature's fertilizer engine for the soil.

This means it is hard to over-apply and the application rates are very flexible and forgiving.

Compost acts like a pro-biotic health tonic for your soil. It will help balance many of the problems that we have with soil. It helps clay soil to drain while helping sand to hold water. It will balance PH. It will help clay to be less compacted and sand to hold together better. And it acts like a sponge or magnet to hold the nutrients in your soil so they can be effective. If you add lime to your compost pile it will multiply its effectiveness on the soil by 50x!

While your soil may be lacking specific nutrients it is always best to start with a foundation of compost and then see if you need to do anything else later.

Not all Compost is Created Equal

Because good compost is more than just black rotted stuff there are different grades. It will only be as good as the ingredients it is made from and the levels of microbes in it. If you buy composted manure in a plastic bag, it will have some value but will lack the nutritional diversity of compost made with manure and diverse plant material and stored where the microbes won't suffocate. Compost made by just piling stuff up and letting it rot will be good but could still contain weed seeds or pathogens if it doesn't get hot enough.

Danger! Killer Compost

There is a growing problem among gardeners with chemical contamination in compost. Many people spray herbicides on pastures or lawns that don't kill grasses but kill broadleaf plants. This makes for a nice-looking lawn or pasture, but the herbicides are very persistent and if you make compost from grass that has been sprayed or manure from animals that have eaten that grass it can hurt or kill many of your plants in your garden. Check your sources and grow your own compost material if possible.

HOW DO YOU MAKE COMPOST ON A HOMESTEAD SCALE?

Why Should You Make Your Own Compost?

One of the things that motivates gardeners and homesteaders is resiliency. We grow our own food because we don't want to rely on unreliable supply chains and fragile industrial systems. But to produce home-grown vegetables and fruits sustainably we also need home-grown compost. And we need a lot of it! Purchasing quality compost is very expensive and keeps us dependent. But it is not hard to make your own. You just need a simple system for making large quantities. That is what you will learn in this booklet.

Different Composting Techniques

Composting involves organic material rotting through decomposition by aerobic (needs oxygen) bacteria. It can be as simple as piling up material and letting it rot over several years before using it. But there are benefits to picking a system that works for you. Here are three main approaches to making compost:

1. **Static Composting:** This method involves building a pile of diverse materials like leaves, grass, manure, woodchips, and kitchen scraps and letting it sit 'static', until everything is decomposed. Optionally the pile may be

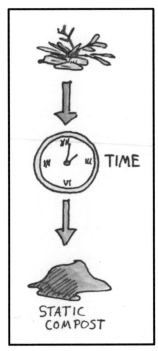

STATIC COMPOST

turned sometime during the process to add air and mix the material. The benefit of this method is that it can be done in a small space, takes very little effort, and is very simple. The disadvantages are that it takes a long time and does not kill weed seeds that may be in the pile. Small, backyard compost barrels or other composting devices can help speed up the process through aerating the material to encourage decomposition.

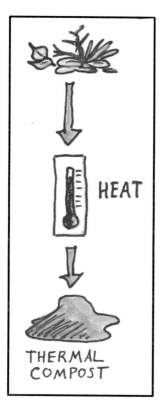

2. **Thermal Composting:** This method involves building a pile that creates the ideal conditions for the aerobic microbes to decompose the material and maintaining those conditions by turning the pile. The benefits of this method are that it is fast (8 weeks), gets the material hot enough to kill any weed seeds, and creates a consistent, reliable product. The disadvantages are that it takes a lot of material to make a pile and requires more labor to turn it.

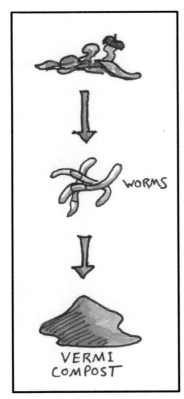

3. **Vermicompost:** Vermicompost uses worms to make compost. This method is great for urban settings because it can be done in a very small area and utilizes kitchen scraps. All you need is a container in which you feed the worms, and there are many different designs you can choose from. If you have a drain at the bottom, you can drain off the very valuable 'worm tea' that makes an amazing fertilizer. The disadvantage of this system is that it requires a bit more on-going management to keep the worms happy.

Thermal Compost: The Most Reliable System

Thermal composting is one of the best systems for reliably producing enough compost for a homestead. With this method the decomposition heats the materials in the pile to speed up the breakdown and kill any unwanted weed seeds. The result is a very consistent, uniform product from pile to pile. It will allow you to make enough compost to use as a reliable substitute for fertilizer. One 4x4x4 ft pile per season should be enough for the needs of a 400 square foot intensive vegetable garden, or one quarter acre of corn.

Here are the steps you need to take to make your own thermal compost pile:

1. Gather Your Materials
2. Assemble Your Compost Pile
3. Monitor Your Compost
4. Turn Your Pile
5. Age Your Compost
6. Use Your Compost!

STEP ONE: GATHER YOUR MATERIALS

Materials Needed To Make Thermal Compost

There are four types of materials that we need to collect:

Green Material (45% of pile):

This is any plant material that is cut while still green. It contains the sugars that will feed the bacteria we want to grow in our pile. Examples of this include grass clipping or hay, green leaves from trees, green weeds, and green crop residue like green tomato vines. The green in the plant indicates the presence of sugar and when we cut the material it traps the sugars in it, which stay present even if the material turns brown. That is why we say, 'cut green'. Grass hay for animals is often brown, but it is a green material because it was green when it was cut.

Brown Material (40% of pile):

This is any plant material that was brown before it was cut or collected. It contains the carbon that the fungus we want to grow like to feed on.

Examples of brown material are fall leaves, straw, dead plant stalks, and small woodchips.

Woody Material (5% of pile):

This is brown material that is chunky to help give the pile structure and keep it aerated.

Examples include large branches, stalks, chunky wood chips, and pinecones.

Nitrogen Material (10%-20% of pile):

We need nitrogen to help fuel the bacteria as they break down the pile. This can include manure from animals not fed sprayed pasture or hay, and leaves and stalks from  leguminous plants like beans and peas. If we use manure, it should be around 10% of the total pile and if we use legumes, they should be around 20% of the total pile. Manure also varies in concentration of nitrogen. The larger the animal the less potent the manure and the smaller the more potent. So, you would need to use more manure from a cow and less from chickens.

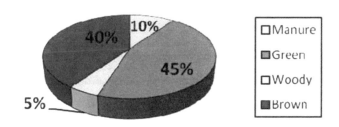

Stockpile Your Materials

Thermal compost piles are built all at once and we don't add anything to them afterwards except water. To work successfully and be worth the effort a thermal compost pile must be a certain size with enough of the material to get hot. The minimum size pile recommended is 4 ft x 4 ft x 4 ft (1.2 m). As we collect materials we don't add them to the compost pile. Instead, we keep them in separate material piles until we accumulate enough to assemble them into a compost pile. Below is an example of stockpile bays.

CHICKENS

GARDEN

NITROGEN

GREEN

BROWN

WOODY

STOCKPILES

COMPOST BAYS

WATER

SAMPLE COMPOST SITE LAYOUT

STEP TWO: ASSEMBLE YOUR COMPOST PILE

Tools and Supplies Needed

- o 6 stakes 5 ft. long (1.5 m long)
- o 2, 50 gal. (200 L) drums or stock tanks for water
- o Pitchforks or digging forks
- o 3 ft. section of thick wire or metal rod

Prep Your Site

For optimal conditions our pile needs to be as cube-shaped as possible. This helps more of the material to be exposed to the heat in the middle. All we need to do to accomplish this is make some simple bays to contain the material. Although you can use wooden sides it is recommended that you just use six simple stakes or posts that are around the same length as the side or height of your pile. Again, the minimum recommended size you should build is 4 ft x 4 ft x 4 ft (1.2 m). If you have a lot of material available and desire double the amount of compost you can save on time and labor by building a bigger, 5'x5'x5' (1.5m), pile.

Build Your Pile

To locate your bays, find an area close to your garden and a water source. You will need an area beside the bins for stockpiling your materials ahead of time. If you are making a 4 ft (1.2 m) pile simply install the stakes in two rows of three with 4 ft (1.2 m) spacing between all the posts. This will give you one bay you can build your pile in and another that you can flip it into.

To build your pile gather a few friends or family to help you. Place two, 50-gallon (200 liter) barrels or trash cans next to the new pile toward the stockpiled material and fill them with water. One barrel will be used to wet green material and the other for brown.

ASSEMBLING YOUR COMPOST PILE

1. LAYOUT STAKES — 4', 4', 4' minimum
2. MANURE → ADD WATER AND MIX
3. BROWN MATERIAL → WATER BARREL → 2-3 INCH LAYER
4. GREEN MATERIAL → WATER → 2-3 INCH LAYER
5. MANURE → 1 INCH LAYER
6. REPEAT LAYERS UNTIL HEIGHT EQUALS WIDTH

Use a wheelbarrow or pile on the ground to mix water into the manure. Begin saturating brown and green material by submerging them in the barrels before placing them in the first square of your bins. To keep your ratios start with a layer (2-3 inches) of brown then add a layer of green, then add a thinner layer of manure. Keep repeating this pattern until you reach the desired height. Don't forget to add some woody material in the brown layers.

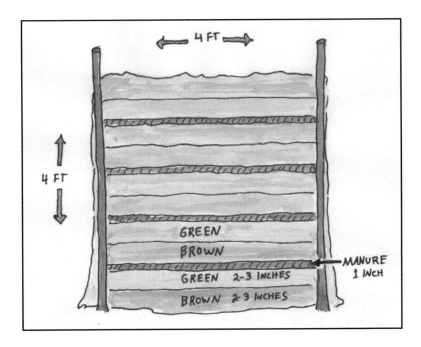

To ensure a nice square pile pay attention to building up the corners and don't let it get high in the middle. This is a great opportunity to apply high standards! Top off your pile with some long grass to help shed water if it is rainy. Don't put plastic over your pile unless it is suspended or this can keep the pile from getting oxygen.

STEP THREE: MONITOR YOUR PILE

Monitoring Temperature

We will flip our pile based on temperature, not just time. Use a simple piece of thick wire or metal rod inserted into the center of your pile to monitor the heat. Check the temperature of your pile by removing the rod and feeling the end. If you can't hold it for more than five seconds you know that your pile is at the ideal temperature (130-150 Fahrenheit, 55-68 Celsius). At the point that it reaches that temperature (typically 1-3 days after building) you need to wait three days. Then you will turn your pile into the next bay.

After turning, monitor the temperature again and once it reaches the right temperature wait another three days then turn. Ideally you will reach that temperature peak three to four times before the pile begins to cool.

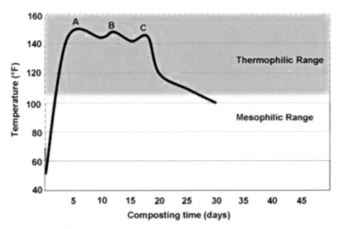

Monitoring Moisture

When you turn you should check and see if you need to add any water. As the pile cooks it will lose water through steam and could dry out. Squeeze a handful of material from the center of the pile and then open your hand. If the material falls apart it is too dry, and you should add water as you turn. If the material stays together, it is the ideal moisture. If the material squishes water out when squeezed it is too wet and turning will help dry it out.

Keep Records

Use a calendar or the compost record sheet at the end of this booklet for keeping records of observations for each compost pile you build. It will help you keep track of each pile and improve your management. For fun you can give each compost pile a name. Then you can tell your kids to go "check Larry's temperature!".

STEP FOUR: TURN YOUR COMPOST

Turning your compost pile is simple. Just use a fork to move all the material from one section of four posts to the adjacent section made up of the two unused posts and two middle posts. Try to rotate the pile so the outside material moves to the inside and the inside has a turn on the outside. *Do not try to maintain the initial layers.* Add water while turning if needed.

To keep a good cube shape, build the corners and sides and keep the center from mounding up by pulling it out to the edges. Record the turn on your calendar and re-insert your temperature rod.

What if my compost doesn't get hot?

Most likely this is an indicator of not enough nitrogen. Try adding some more wet nitrogen material while turning the pile. This will set the calendar for your pile back to day one of the eight-week process because you have added fresh material. Another reason for not attaining the proper heat would be if the pile got too dry causing the microbes to go dormant.

STEP FIVE: AGE YOUR COMPOST

After your pile begins cooling it is not as critical to flip it. The fungus that begins working in the pile after it cools down prefers to not be disrupted too much. But it is advisable to still turn every week or two in order to maintain proper moisture and add air. Normally you will turn your pile a total of 7-9 times. After 8 weeks from initially building the pile, it will be ready to use. However, it will keep and continue to age until you need it. Don't store your pile near trees or the roots will invade it.

STEP SIX: USE YOUR COMPOST!

Options for Compost Application

Broadcast on Bed

For your initial application on a garden, you should apply a generous layer of compost if possible. If you can afford it and have enough compost, broadcast it on the top of your garden beds at the rate of 1 wheelbarrow load per 20 square ft of garden bed (1.8 square meters). If you want to use 5 gal. (20 L) buckets, five buckets are equivalent to one wheelbarrow load. The average 4x4x4 thermal compost pile will cover 140 square feet at this rate, the equivalent of 7 wheelbarrows of compost. Subsequent yearly applications are recommended and will require around half the initial rate. Rake the compost level and evenly across the surface of the bed.

Apply in Planting Hole

If you have a limited amount of compost, save it to apply directly in the planting hole or furrow when you plant.

On-Going Fertility

After initial installation of your garden, compost is applied prior to each planting of heavy feeding crops. This can be broadcast over the bed at the rate of up to three 5-gallon (20 liter) buckets 20 square ft of garden bed (1.8 square meters). Or it can be added in the furrow or hole at planting.

Top-Dressing Plants While Growing

Most plants will benefit from a top up of nutrients 4-6 weeks after planting (except for carrots, beans and peas, and onions). Top dressing can be in the form of compost applied around the base of the plants, or added in the form of a fertilizer tea applied at the base of the plant.

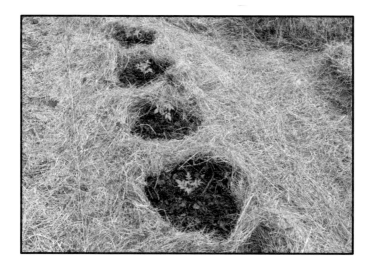

Use Sifted Compost for Starting Seedlings

Use aged, sifted compost as the sole growing medium for starting seedlings in place of expensive potting mix. It works great and produces healthy plants!

BONUS: FERTILIZER TEAS

✓ Fertilizer Tea materials
  - Buckets or drums with lids.
  - Porous sacks
  - Chicken Manure
  - Comfrey or Sunflower Leaves
  - Compost

Compost is a great foundation for our garden's soil fertility, but how do we make sure our plants have all the nutrients they need for uninterrupted growth? Simple, organic fertilizer teas are a great way to provide a boost of nutrients directly to our plants. This is especially helpful if we are lacking enough compost to apply generously on our whole garden.

Here are three simple teas that are helpful to learn how to make:

Chicken Manure Tea – Leaf growth

This tea is used to supply nitrogen and helps our plants grow a lot of leaves. To make chicken manure tea simply place 60-90 lbs. (30-40 kgs) of chicken manure into a porous bag like a plastic feed sack and suspend it in a 50-gallon (200 liter) drum for 3 weeks, stirring regularly. To eliminate smell, add lactic acid bacteria by adding a cup of the clear liquid whey that separates from yogurt. To use, dilute 1 part tea to 10 parts water. Apply at a rate of 1.5 cups (350 ml) per plant or per 2 feet (60 cm) of row to the soil only. DO NOT APPLY TO LEAVES. This tea can be saved and does not have to be used all at once.

Comfrey Tea – Fruit Production

This tea is used to supply extra potassium and support fruit production. Collect 2-4 lbs (1-2 kg) of comfrey (also sunflower leaves or banana peels) and submerge them in a 5 gallon (20 liter) bucket. Cover them and let them sit, stirring regularly for 2-4 weeks, depending on how warm the weather is. To use, dilute 1 part tea to 20 parts water and apply to the leaves or soil around fruiting plants like tomatoes and peppers. Potatoes also benefit from comfrey tea. This tea can be saved and does not have to be used all at once.

Compost Tea – General Plant health

This tea is used to add microbial life to the soil or plant leaves and support their general health. It can help prevent disease and pests. Take 8 lbs (4kg) of good quality compost for a 5-gallon (20 liter) bucket and use a porous bag to suspend it in water for 7 days, stirring regularly. You want to use it all at once because it is living, and the microbes will die if you store it. To use, dilute one part compost tea to 20 parts water and apply to leaves and soil around plants.

Rule of thumb: Apply top dressing every 2 weeks where appropriate.

- **Manure tea** is only applied at the base of plants that need **LEAF** growth.
- **Comfrey or sunflower tea** is applied foliarly or on the soil to support **FRUIT** production (tomato, pepper, etc.)
- **Compost tea** is applied foliarly or to soil for all plants to encourage **general HEALTH**.
- Every two weeks you can alternate applying one of these fertilizers on the appropriate plants. For example:
  - Week 2. Chicken manure tea at the base of cabbage, corn, and kale plants (do not get on leaves).
  - Week 4. Comfrey tea on Tomato, Pepper, and Squash plants.
  - Week 6. Compost tea on all plants.

CONCLUSION: BUILDING COMMUNITY THROUGH COMPOST

Don't compost alone! As you learn to make compost on your homestead, invite family members and neighbors to help in return for some compost. It is a great community event. As you experience success and increase in your skill embrace the responsibility of passing on what you know. You will find that your joy in making compost will grow as you share it with others!

COMPOST RECORD SHEET

Action	Date	Comments
Build		
1st Turn		
2nd Turn		
3rd Turn		
4th Turn		
5th Turn		
6th Turn		
7th Turn		
8th Turn		
9th Turn		

COMPOST RECORD SHEET

Action	Date	Comments
Build		
1st Turn		
2nd Turn		
3rd Turn		
4th Turn		
5th Turn		
6th Turn		
7th Turn		
8th Turn		
9th Turn		

COMPOST RECORD SHEET

Action	Date	Comments
Build		
1st Turn		
2nd Turn		
3rd Turn		
4th Turn		
5th Turn		
6th Turn		
7th Turn		
8th Turn		
9th Turn		

OTHER LINKS AND RESOURCES:

Foundations for Farming

Foundations for Farming Zimbabwe

www.foundationsforfarming.org

Foundations for Farming USA

www.redeemingthedirt.com

The Well-Watered Garden Project

www.wellwateredgardenproject.org

Online Agricultural Training and Mentoring

www.redeemingthedirtacademy.com

Homestead-Scale Compost Video Course on the School of Traditional Skills

If you want to learn more about making your own compost for your homestead using the simple system outlined in this booklet, check out my video course on the online School of Traditional Skills. Use the QR code below to support us through our affiliate link.

Trailer Video for Class